MW00649266

How To Survive Your Quarter Life Crisis

JODANNA BIRD

© Copyright 2018 by Jodanna Bird

Cover design and illustrations by Jodanna Bird

All rights reserved. No part of this publication may be reproduced, stored in a retrieval system or transmitted, in any form or by any means, without the prior written permission of the author, nor be otherwise circulated in any form of binding or cover other than that in which it is published and without a similar condition being imposed on the subsequent purchaser.

The information in this book is designed to provide helpful information on the subjects discussed. This book is not meant to be used, nor should it be used, to diagnose or treat any psychological or medical condition. References are provided for informational purposes only and do not constitute endorsement of any websites or other sources. Readers should be aware that the websites listed in this book were live and correct at the time of writing and may change. If any of the references are found to be incorrect, please notify the author who will amend the information immediately.

www.jodannabird.com

First published in December 2018.

ISBN 978-1-9993717-0-8
eISBN 978-1-9993717-1-5

To anyone who feels lost

Contents

Foreword

Hello and welcome to your quarter-life crisis.

Let me guess: you've dyed your hair purple and can't decide how to ask your boss for a 'find yourself' sabbatical.

No purple hair? Good. I got here just in time.

I'll cut to the chase.

Yes, a quarter-life crisis *is* a thing. No, you are not on your own.

Heck, I think I've been going through my quarter-life crisis for six years, since I left higher education at the age of 22. It's difficult getting turfed out into the big wide world without a timetable. How am I supposed to function without knowing I have Maths on Wednesday and PE to avoid on Thursday? Why don't the Teacher Gods give us lessons on how to find a job that doesn't suck and sustain a relationship for longer than the legendary honeymoon period? It's funny, really. We're all in the same 'growing old' boat, but this adulting situation is hard to master. They want to test me on how to calculate Pythagoras' Theorem, but when I'm scratching my head at a random rush of emotions (Saturday morning well spent, crying into my pillow for absolutely NO reason), the formula for any sort of logic has vanished quicker than my three ex-boyfriends.

Alas, fear not. After regular quarter-life crisis updates from my closest friends and a quick scroll through Twitter, I realised that this pandemic is greater than I ever imagined. Not one to miss a golden opportunity, I decided to dig that library card out and bury my brains in a few books. Months of research, conversations with peers and unleashing my own personal experiences has led me to craft this tried and tested method for surviving a quarter-life crisis.

So, before you quit your job, shave your head and book a one-way flight to Phuket (I know, the Phuket Bucket is calling out for you), let's spend a few hours together to see if we can find a bit of logic behind why you feel the way you currently do. Deep breaths. I'm about to take you on an existential journey through the inner workings of that confused head of yours, and together we are going to kiss goodbye to your quarter-life crisis with enough sass to make even Britney feel embarrassed. (You get to keep your hair, too.)

Ready? Great. Let's embark on your self-help journey of a lifetime. And remember, as Zac Efron once sang in *High School Musical*, "We're all in this together".

INTRO

Let me take a wild guess. You're stuck in a job you hate, wondering how everyone else is affording to travel the world while you can barely afford to pay your rent. Is everyone around you having babies and getting married, yet you're still figuring out how to be sexy on Bumble? Are you terrified at the prospect of growing old and wasting your most precious years living a life you don't actually enjoy? Maybe you are just utterly bored with the path you are walking along and you're curious to see what else is out there. According to research, the majority of millennials believe that they are going through a quarter-life crisis.[1] This means that a huge number of us are suffering an epidemic that seems to be widely joked about but barely taken seriously.

The more I listen out for it, the more I hear the magnitude of the quarter-life crisis problem. We pass this phrase around like a hot potato, yet nobody seems to actually be doing anything about it. People in their 40s can't help because they're busy going through their own midlife crisis, and anyone who feels they do have their shit together is content in their own steaming bathtub

15

of self-admiration. As a young adult in your 20s, society expects you to grab life by the balls and enjoy some of your most care-free years, but most of us have unwillingly turned freedom into stress by believing that the way we navigate this decade is crucial for defining what's to follow. We look at our parents and desperately want to make sure we meet or exceed their level of happiness. The pressure is *real*. Some of us have been burdened with more life responsibilities than we deserve, seemingly limiting the things we feel we can actually go out and achieve. Others are just stabbing in the dark until they hit a random target. Most of us are crazily concerned about money to the point of hindrance. We all know that happiness is our ultimate goal; we just don't know what the bloody hell happiness looks like and how on earth to get there. Most importantly, we are hugely grateful for the opportunities we have available to us and don't want to f*ck things up.

This book is the brainchild of many hours of committed reading, learning, exploring, asking, challenging, listening, pondering, understanding and writing. Through the following pages, you will start to learn what a quarter-life crisis actually is, the different circumstances that can trigger it and how to survive it. I will break down, step by step, the phases you need to walk through in order to navigate your way to happiness. I will explain the attitudes and behaviours you should wear like armour for your survival journey, and equip you with research by psychologists, philosophers and neuroscientists for extra support. And finally, I will introduce you to some genuine case studies so that you never feel alone in your suffering. By the end of this book, you will feel reassured about your situation and be excited to move forward into a bright and happy future.

CHAPTER ONE

We all want to be happy, right? Day by day we may fall into a routine of working, eating and sleeping, but in the long term, we are all foraging to find happiness. The problem for us millennials, and the generations that follow us, is that our quest for happiness has many annoying digital distractions. The whole world is our audience, causing us to be constantly fixated on how successful and happy we appear to be on social media, with most of us likely to win awards for our acting skills. But few of us are really knowledgeable about what truly makes us happy. Just think about it for one second. Do you genuinely, hand on heart, 100 percent know what makes you happy? Can you seriously answer that question right now without hesitation? (No. Weekend-long binges of *Gossip Girl* don't count. Not even if they re-write the ending.) If you can answer that question *honestly* right now, are you actively making the important life decisions that will set you up to achieve your goals? If you can't answer that question, why not?

Either way, I think we can all sit here and say that we tend to be far more concerned with trying to *act* happy (and photograph the sentiment for the world to see) rather than genuinely *being* happy. You know that cliché phrase, 'It's one for the gram'? How many times have you been somewhere or done something massively mediocre, yet you stop to get a killer photo for your Instagram so that your entire social sphere thinks your life is great? What's more, I don't think this behavioural habit is one that our generation is particularly ashamed of. I mean, we all know what each other is doing, don't we? Having spoken to various friends about the idea of showboating fake happiness rather than seeking genuine happiness, they have freely admitted that a significant part of their recent lives has been dedicated to appearing happy and successful on social media, when in fact they are pretty miserable with the reality that they are trying to live. In this digital world of influencer culture, and 'follower' counts being a currency of their own, it is almost impossible to ignore what everyone else is doing and to resist the temptation to visually compete with them. Isn't it a sad truth that in this instance we are actually all competing for nothing?

The nature of *acting* happy rather than *being* happy means that we are *reacting* rather than *researching*. We are all victims of many difficult life scenarios and tend to make our key decisions as a result of them. We obsess over the images we see online and hope that we will feel happy if we imitate the digital façade of appearing to be happy. Instead, we should spend our time looking inward and digging deeper to discover what personal values will truly make us happy, and then prioritise those values. We can only be truly happy if we know exactly what will make us happy and strive to obtain that ideal.

As we are all made up of different DNA and raised in different environments, our wants and needs are completely independent of each other, so the incorrect fallacy that emulating one another's online presence – posting holiday pictures or boasting about a recent promotion – will bring us digital recognition is a cheap fix for a fundamental human need. But don't feel too bad, it's not entirely your fault. Silicon Valley giants know exactly how to manipulate your brain for their own financial gain. What once started as literal social media has now undeniably become savvy business, and our mental well-being is, unfortunately, caught in the crossfire. The reward sensation we feel when we receive likes, followers or complimentary comments online is somewhere in the region of a drug addiction that we cannot seem to shake.[2] A powerful chemical called dopamine is released into our brains whenever we experience these types of successful social interactions. It is the same chemical that is active when we have sex, exercise and eat incredible food, and it is responsible for many of our learning behaviours. But it is a dangerous notion to believe that we can rely entirely on these short outbursts of pleasure when trying to achieve genuine happiness. It is also naïve to think that acting happy online will make you happy offline. Time and again, researchers have proven that the more we use social media, the more we suffer feelings of loneliness, depression, distractedness and sleep disturbances.[3] There are so many reasons why it is beneficial to back away from social media and cleanse our souls with a digital detox, or at least establish a better balance between the two. What I am most interested in studying is how breaking the habit of cheap thrills and spending more time self-reflecting will steer you through your quarter-life crisis (QLC).

Research has suggested that happiness is the result of a combination of both pleasure *and* purpose over a significant period of time.[4] This reinforces the notion that digital recognition alone is not enough to sustain our happiness and prevent us from suffering a QLC. It is too short term. In fact, our continual engagement with the digital world is exhausting our energy and brain power, meaning we are wasting valuable time that could otherwise be invested into flourishing within a more deeply satisfying journey. In its simplest sense, the pleasure principle of social media engagement is encouraging us to become lazy with regards to looking after our own happiness and well-being. Eventually, when our pleasure principle (the digital world) dramatically changes or perhaps even ceases to exist, where will that leave our mental well-being? It's a scary thought.

What if we were to change our tactics? What if we invested our time into inward thinking and self-assessment rather than seeking the approval of strangers? Instead of feeling happiness and excitement because a complete stranger from a distant country 'liked' our latest Instagram post and subsequently took our follower count from 99 to 100 (a nice round number – what a milestone!), what if we had the power to feel happiness at any moment we needed it? Isn't it a smarter idea to train our brains to feel happiness from activities and achievements that we have identified as truly important to us, and are in full control over, rather than relying on computers and the opinions of others? Putting our happiness into the hands of unreliable and uncaring sources is an emotional death trap. Putting our happiness into our own hands, however, and learning to continually look after it despite negative external events, is surely the way to go.

So, what exactly is a QLC? We all form expectations and plans for what we hope to achieve in our lives. Sometimes our plans are created from a young age and are based on our parents, passions or educational successes, and other times our expectations are based on what everyone else around us seems to be doing, including social norms and conventional pressure. More often than not, we form our expectations as a result of haphazard probing by other people, forcing us to panic and vocalise false ideals in a bid to appear like we have our shit together. Have you ever been sat in a job interview and asked the nauseating question, "Where do you see yourself in five years' time?" Now I'm a pretty driven person, but even I get flustered trying to tackle that nonsensical prediction. Sure, some god-like beings might have their #lifegoals written down on paper somewhere, but most of us feel like we make this shit up as we go along. I guess the problem is that from time to time we perform our own personal spot checks to see if we have achieved what we wanted in life by a certain age. Most likely, the spot check will be conducted in our subconscious mind (where the majority of our mental activities are performed), so as not to disturb our essential daily routines. More often than not, the spot check occurs long before we realise, allowing negative feelings of unrest to manifest until they eventually come to fruition in our conscious mind.[5] That's the reason why some QLC sufferers may struggle to pinpoint the exact moment their QLC began. Usually, there are deep-rooted underlying problems in our thoughts that fester until an external incident forces our conscious mind to pay attention. And then, ta da! Welcome to the world, pesky QLC. The dramatic conscious realisation that we are not quite where we had planned to be by a certain age or moment in our life sends us into meltdown mode – a state of panic with huge uncertainty about our future. Depression can enter the mix, with feelings of failure and worthlessness. We compare our lives to those around us and can't understand why everything is so easy for them and so difficult for us. Overall, it's a pretty scary sensation that can leave us completely lost and confused, or spur us on to behave in erratic and uncontrollable ways. Ultimately, a quarter-life crisis is when you feel you are not meeting the expectations you had for your life, sending you into a state of confusion and feeling loss of control.

Ok, let's be honest, most of us who have suffered a QLC simply ended up quitting our jobs and moving abroad (guilty!), but these bold life changes may not truly help us to understand or survive our QLC. In fact, continual job-hopping, moving abroad, serial dating and extravagant purchases are all just short-term fixes for a deeper-rooted problem. It's perhaps not quite as short term as the social media recognition fix, but it's not a million miles from it. Instead, we need to pin down the *real* way to survive a QLC. We need a tried and tested series of actions that will ensure that we are confident, clear and prepared for our new journey to happiness.

The idea of a QLC isn't really a new one. For instance, think about the original 'midlife crisis'. It's the exact same thing, just a bit later in life when we have a few more wrinkles and a bit more baggage. We usually associate the term 'midlife crisis' with middle-aged folk who quit their corporate jobs to become bakers, get a divorce and drink themselves into oblivion. But over and above that, there is plenty of significant research in existence that explores concepts that could be deemed similar to the QLC, mainly those that study human happiness and how to achieve it. For me, solving a QLC involves a bit more than figuring out how to be happy, though. A QLC sufferer has misaligned expectations for their own life, and they need to first understand exactly *what* they want in order to create new goals that they can set out to achieve. Only at this point can the quest for happiness ensue.

Let's get deep for a minute and consider the work of Carl Gustav Jung, a prolific writer and psychologist who spent a valuable amount of time in the early 1900s studying and developing our understanding of the human personality. In particular, Jung is responsible for our use of the terms *introvert* and *extrovert*, but one of his most major contributions to the field of psychology is in his studies of adult development. Unlike his peer, Freud, who placed emphasis on the past and held childhood experiences accountable for the way that our adult personalities develop, Jung was mostly interested in how adults who had identified a dissatisfaction with their lives could actively change it through digging deep to understand the self. He placed great emphasis on his patients understanding themselves as individuals and focussing on their future.[6] What I love about Jung's theories is that he firmly believed that we are all capable of moulding and shaping ourselves in order to improve our lives. Although Jung did appreciate Freudian theories, he did not believe that we can 'shirk' our adult problems onto our childhood. We can't hold our upbringing accountable for our future behaviours. Instead, he placed emphasis on the concept that we should all strive to have our own personalities. He described personality as *"an adult ideal"*.[7] This adult ideal really resonates with me. QLC sufferers have lost sight of their individuality, doubted their personality or become confused about their adult ideal. They may even blame their external circumstances for the position they find themselves in, but Jung's theories favour those who are determined to accept their unhappiness and work to change it. Ultimately, we are all malleable and capable of redefining our path, no matter what difficult situation we find ourselves in. The power to create a life we love is entirely in our own hands. It is this ability to continually strive for improvement that will allow us to survive our QLC. Exciting, huh?

A QLC could be compared to an existential crisis. This makes sense when thinking about Jung's theories, which focus on the need for adults to develop their own personalities and ideals. The symptoms are somewhat similar; sufferers question the meaning of life and their individual purpose.[8] My friends all know that my theory of happiness has always been to find your purpose. There have been many times that those closest to me have confided in me that they feel miserable, lost and confused. Whenever we sit down together to discuss the potential causes for their anxiety or depression, we always realise that the problems arose when their considered reason for existence was suddenly no longer identifiable. Maybe they broke up with their boyfriend, lost their job, or their dog Ted sadly died. Note that I used the word 'considered' here. I strongly believe that, more often than not, we falsely identify our reason for existence, so when (for some reason) that job, person or passion no longer exists in our lives, we fall into a QLC. But what will begin to unfold through the pages of this book is that our true purpose is yet to be realised, and that this entire time we may have been chasing an incorrect adult ideal. In a QLC, life is telling us that it is time for a change. Our predetermined road to happiness is not the right one anymore, so now we find ourselves at a big crossroads. The beauty of this is that the move we're about to make, and subsequently the future of our happiness, is a decision that lies entirely in our own hands.

CHAPTER ONE — TAKEAWAYS

- A QLC happens when you feel you are not meeting the expectations you had for your life, sending you into a state of confusion and feeling loss of control.
- A QLC is a positive opportunity for you to change the path that you have found yourself on.
- In order to successfully change your path, you need to look inward and identify what your purpose is.
- Scaling back the use of social media will significantly help with your ability to focus on inward thinking.
- Surviving a QLC is completely possible and entirely within your own hands.

CHAPTER TWO

WHY?

In the previous chapter, I defined a QLC as feelings of anxiety and confusion caused by performing a spot check on your life and realising that you are not where you thought you would be at that particular moment or age. Most QLC sufferers feel that the *reason* for their QLC is because they can't find a job they love. Many others believe that their anxieties are provoked by comparing themselves to other people of the same age and feeling inadequate. A large number of sufferers are stressed by financial concerns, or feel pressure from their parents to marry and have a baby.

To me, these scenarios are all common examples of negative thoughts that a sufferer may feel simultaneous to the realisation of their QLC, but the actual *trigger* of a QLC is yet to be identified. For instance, why are human beings the only living organisms prone to this experience? Why do humans bother to think so deeply about why they are failing to achieve an intangible utopia, rather than only focussing on primitive survival tasks? My hamster doesn't have this stress. Why?!

Ancient Greek philosophers spent years defining the functions of humans and other living beings such as plants and animals. Aside from sharing fundamental life requirements, such as growing, using energy and reproducing, human beings have the superior capability of using reason and language to pursue meaningful and rational endeavours. The choices we make as humans combined with our ability to *imagine* is what makes us who we are, and sets us apart from all other living things. Imagination is one element of our mind that contributes to the creation of our own ideals, or what I have previously termed as the expectations we have for our own lives. In his book *Your Mind and How to Use It*, psychologist William Walker Atkinson writes, "The influence of our ideals is perceived to affect not only our character but also our place and degree of success in life".[9] Put simply, human beings have been gifted a brain structure that allows us to think in a much more sophisticated way than any other living being on the planet. Through combinations of perception, memory, imagination and many more complex brain functions, we are able to design our own individual pathways and reinvent our future time and time again. The trouble is, if our ideals are unidentifiable, or unsatisfactory, we will mark ourselves as unsuccessful. This spurs on feelings of anxiety and stress.

Transferring this philosophy to a more practical process, imagine that life is a game and you are a character within that game. *The Sims* (circa 2000) is the perfect example. *Cue sighs of nostalgia*. When you create your avatar in *The Sims*, you are able to choose your appearance and personality attributes, but most interestingly you are also prompted to choose what your life 'aspiration' should be. This then determines the long-term actions of your Sim, giving the game a purpose and narrative. In the original version of *The Sims*, the aspiration options were knowledge, fortune, popularity, romance or family. Whichever aspiration you chose would spark a series of events that would encourage your Sim to strive to achieve goals. For example, if your aspiration was popularity, you would often receive visits from neighbours and your purpose would be to socialise with them, host parties and visit them in return. Eventually, your social profile would boom and you would become a Sim celebrity. When your Sim neglected the daily goals required to build on the aspiration, they would become stressed, and no matter how fancy you built their house or how big you made their swimming pool, their general purpose would eventually become non-existent. But as with any game, there was an option to change and adapt this aspiration as time went on. More often than not, I would get bored with trying to be popular and instead pursue the knowledge aspiration so that I could become a wealthy working professional and get picked up in a cool car every morning. Whichever route I picked, though, if I pursued it for long enough my Sim would be happy with their success, and as a result everything else in the game would flow.

We human beings have the opportunity to create our own epic journey, and to recreate the journey if for some reason the original plan falls short. We have the luxury of *imagination* and can do whatever the hell we want with it. Our life is a blank canvas. We can paint absolutely anything. It can be meticulously crafted or unpredictable and expressive. We can start painting in one style and then suddenly change to another. Art is subjective; there is no right or wrong. Most importantly, the process of painting a picture is more valuable to us than the physicality of the final piece. So, let's not consider the QLC as a symbol of failure, but more positively, as a sign of guidance. Imagine Pablo Picasso is your mentor. He knows what you want to achieve, but can see that your technique is slightly off. He will interject for reasons that don't immediately seem obvious, but as time goes on it will make perfect sense. Sometimes you have no idea of the picture you want to paint. Picasso will force you to figure that out. This is the reason for your QLC. Life/God/Picasso (however you want to look at it) is helping you to see that it is time for change. The following life experiences are common examples of how you will be probed to reassess your plan.

BURNOUT

Earlier this year I was working in the advertising industry in London, juggling two other freelance projects alongside my full-time job to fund my crazy West London rent and a couple of holidays. In addition to work, I was trying to manage a long-distance relationship with a French guy (a story I look forward to divulging in book #2), as well as sustaining a healthy social life with my friends and family. During the summer, I slowly found myself feeling very uninspired and disconnected from work – something that seemed quite strange for me as I'm a textbook workaholic. Days passed, and I began to get paranoid that I was forgetting everything my friends were telling me about their lives. Usually I'm a brilliant listener, so this caused alarm bells to ring. I had a job interview lined up and obliviously arrived an hour late. It was a 'worst nightmare' scenario, receiving a phone call from an angry interviewer whilst sat on the tube merrily enjoying my *'Friday Feels'* playlist. What really raised suspicions, though, was when I had a sudden and quite serious break out of psoriasis. Weird red spots flared up all over my body (kind of like a Dalmatian gone wrong). Having always been a positive, punctual and well-balanced person (with very good skin!), I eventually realised that something strange was happening. Despite my queries, I continued to push myself physically and mentally because I refused to accept that I was unable to cope with my life – the life that I was lucky to live. "How can I be *that* stressed?" I thought. "I live in a lovely house, with incredibly supportive friends. My family is healthy and my finances are fine." I had convinced myself that it would be pathetic and embarrassing to admit defeat when so many other people in the world are suffering much worse than me. My grandparents had survived a World War and I couldn't even survive my 9-5? So I pushed any weak thoughts out of my mind to prove that I was not a victim, but it wasn't too long after that when the scales tipped and I fell physically ill with some sort of infection. My whole body was in pain. I could barely muster the energy to walk. My mood was erratic, causing me to unpredictably burst into tears at any moment of the day. The thought of facing work, my employers and day-to-day situations caused waves of anxiety to crash aggressively through my brain. Flustered by the routine e-mail demands I was receiving from my employers, I waved a white flag and forced myself to stay home for a week. I buried myself under blankets and binged on every Netflix series I could find. I visited the doctor and had blood tests. I ate more fruit and vegetables than can be found at Borough Market. In the days that proceeded, I slowly built myself back up emotionally and physically until I felt healthy enough to return to regular life. What I learned on my return was that the companies I worked for hadn't imploded or collapsed. No one was angry or annoyed that I had been away for a while. The guilt I had felt for staying home to calm down was unnecessary. But what was necessary, I realised, was the burnout. I had ignored every single one of my wake-up calls. I had continued to push my mind and body past my personal limit at that particular moment until life had to take over and force me to stop. "It's time for a change," life said. *Cue my very own QLC.*

In the months that followed, I began to make changes to my routine. It was hard, but I had to accept that I couldn't be everything to everyone. I couldn't be the perfect employee to three different employers at the same time. I couldn't be fully present in the most romantic relationship of my life with a man from another country. I couldn't be fully involved with my friends and family in the way that I truly wanted. But most importantly, I couldn't even look after my own health. Burnout can be many things to many different people, but for me, burnout is a wake-up call. It's a big fat flashing beacon of light, forcing us to sit down and reassess our life plan. It's a sign that we're wandering aimlessly in the wrong direction and the only way that we will realise it is by force. And for me, it worked. I scaled everything back, I identified what was important to me, and I pivoted to a new life plan that involved completely relocating and pursuing something much more meaningful. Sure, there were sacrifices. HUGE sacrifices. But now I understand the system, and I trust it.

Half a million UK employees have reported suffering burnout.[10] That's a bloody huge statistic! We are living in a society that seems to praise those that work around the clock and shame those that show signs of weakness. Most people are pressurised into feeling that leaving the office at 5.30pm on the dot, or arriving bang on 9am, is the attitude of someone who doesn't want to succeed. Being present in the office late at night has been adopted by brag culture to be the behaviour of someone who is working hard, when actually it is a sure-fire route to failure. Personal failure. I don't think we should be competing for the title of 'who works the hardest'. Instead, we should champion those who work the smartest, because ultimately, none of us will be working at all if we burn ourselves out to a point that hinders our health. We are human beings, not machines.

DISSATISFACTION

Have you ever found that you arrive home from work, your key is in the front door, yet you can't recall a single moment from your journey? It's like your mind was completely absent the entire time you moved from A to B. It just mentally checked itself out and left your body to deal with the mundane activity of commuting. It's happened to me many times in the past, mostly when sat in the car (yikes!). My autopilot takes over because my conscious mind is too precious to waste energy on the boring routine that I've created.

This ability to switch into autopilot mode is yet another impressive function of the human brain and essential in ensuring that we are not constantly bamboozled. With between 60,000 and 80,000 thoughts entering our minds each day,[11] our brains are wired to cope by filtering only the significant few into our main, conscious brain. The main part of our brain doesn't need to bother getting involved with tasks such as brushing our teeth, for example. But what happens when our entire lives switch to autopilot? You wake up, go to work, come home, watch TV, go to sleep, do it again tomorrow. This routine is commonly repeated within millions of households around the world, yet most people fail to recognise that forming this routine is not the point of life at all, and in the long term it could be instigating some festering feelings of dissatisfaction in our subconscious. Carl Jung wrote, "Panic is liable to break out among human beings kept unconscious by routine…"[12]. The 'panic' that Jung mentions occurs when you are locked in a routine and then progressive feelings of dissatisfaction occur.

Similar to burnout, dissatisfaction is most likely to be a gradual occurrence. This is why we are often told to occasionally take a different route to work, or consciously pay more attention to our surroundings. When we journey down a beaten track too many times, it becomes a habit and our autopilot mode kicks in. When we fall victim to routine, we often miss out on many of life's most beautiful moments, and as a result we become uninspired and dissatisfied. It could also be argued that those who live their lives within the confines of a permanent routine are also far less mentally prepared for when an inevitable external event suddenly interrupts their flow. We need to remember that we have the power to spice up our lives whenever the hell we want, and it is very important that we utilise this power.

It may be interesting to focus further on one particular element of a daily routine: a job. As the majority of QLC sufferers have blamed a lack of passion for their job as the reason for their QLC experience, perhaps we can pinpoint dissatisfaction as a major trigger. Most people have been led to believe that moving from education to a 9-5 job is a natural progression and sign of success. To deviate from this pre-formulated path would be head-turning and would immediately place us under the scrutiny of those around us. There are, of course, some daring souls who actively defy this journey by travelling or pursuing unorthodox careers. But for the large proportion of people who do follow convention (without consulting their own adult ideals first), there is a high risk of experiencing crippling dissatisfaction at a later date. Even if the average career journey fell within your predetermined idea of what would make you happy, there is a risk that what you imagined the job would be doesn't match the actual reality of the job. Often, we keep our feelings of dissatisfaction to ourselves because on the surface, most other people seem to be perfectly settled within their 9-5. It makes us feel like we are the problem rather than the job. *"If everyone else is perfectly happy with this routine, why aren't I?"* What we need to remember is that every one of us is different, with different ideals. What works for one person will not work for another. We also need to remember that the widespread notion of a 9-5 equalling success is an outdated concept, and we now have the ability to change it. Sometimes, though, we need a little nudge. Cue the QLC.

COMPARING TO OTHERS

Bill Gates and Steve Jobs. Two of the world's greatest tech pioneers. We should probably pay attention to their views on technology and social media, right? After all, between the two of them, they are largely responsible for creating the digital platforms we spend our recent lives fully immersed in. Interestingly, both men limited their children's use of technology. Steve Jobs once prohibited his kids from using the new iPad. Bill Gates didn't allow his children to have mobile phones until they were 14.[13] So what do these two CEOs know that we don't?

Research has found that the risk of depression jumps 27 percent for those that regularly use social media. More research reports that millennials who are addicted to their smartphones get less sleep, feel less connected to their community and feel lonelier.[14] Considering that technology and social media is sold to us as a means of being instantly connected to the rest of the world, isn't it ironic that a large proportion of users are actually feeling less connected? Due to the dopamine addiction I explained earlier, we are chemically hooked on scrolling through the feeds of celebrities, influencers and complete strangers who seem to be perfectly happy and content with their #spon lives. The award-worthy photography, incredible outfits, perfect bikini bodies and locations of a lifetime can be utterly soul destroying when we begin to compare them to our current situation. Most of the time, we are sat at our office desk at 9am on a Monday morning, wondering where our lives went so, so wrong.

Psychologist Mai-Ly Nguyen Steers from the University of Houston refers to this as "everyone else's highlights reel".[15] Essentially, we can't compare the mundane tasks of our everyday life to somebody else's highlights. But I want to explore this even further. Aside from scrolling past the boasting pictures of friends and family, more often than not we are actually looking at a *fictional* reel. Remember that social media platforms are all, first and foremost, businesses.

Earlier this year, I set up a travel blog with a friend to document some of the upcoming journeys we had planned together. We created content and posted our images onto our own Instagram feed and blog website. We discovered that, for the most part, the images that are posted on social media are meticulously crafted, retouched and curated. There are apps specifically designed to pre-plan the entire aesthetic of an Instagram feed before it actually goes live. There are many photographers who are making a substantial living (using expensive equipment) photographing aspiring influencers for their Instagram feeds, whilst we assume that these influencers are doing everything themselves armed with only their mobile phones. Compare this to the months of work, budgets and team members that contribute to major advertising campaigns. Think back to some glamorously iconic ads such as Eva Herzigova's Wonderbra campaign and Kate Moss in Calvin Klein. Essentially, social media is just another business tool being used for marketing products and influencing consumers. Most of the images you see of aspirational people with perfect lives are in fact the result of working with professional teams and financially sponsored posts. Sometimes, as I learned through creating my travel blog, brands approach bloggers to invite them to become a brand ambassador, which simply involves the blogger purchasing a product in order to receive a referral code and the chance of being featured on the brand's page. Even those with minimal followers (we only had 100 followers on our blog when we were invited to do this) are approached. Social media is fast becoming an advertising arena. We may be starting to see an improvement of equal representation across traditional advertising mediums, but unrealistic representations are hiding on social channels in a 'same but different' way. This is why comparing yourself to other people online is a terrible idea. The lines between real and fake are so blurred that you are ultimately setting yourself up for a dramatic fall. Cue your QLC.

TRAUMA

By definition, trauma is a *deeply distressing or disturbing experience*. As with most things in life, the extremity of trauma will vary depending on the person and situation. There is no 'black and white' to trauma; rather, it can exist on any point of a wide spectrum of life-changing events and still have a similar psychological effect. Some may consider the process of divorce to be traumatic, whilst others may be suffering bereavement or a life-changing illness. Each of these situations, no matter how frugal they seem, will leave the victim feeling vulnerable, which then spurs on a set of new behaviours intended to aid the victim with a coping ability. Trauma victims often experience depression and anxiety, and could use alcohol or drugs as a coping mechanism. For some, desperate 'survival' tactics will undoubtedly come into play. This entire chain reaction leads the victim down a dangerous path that will inevitably change their perspective on life.

For 24-year-old Andrew, loss of a close relative was the cause of his life upheaval. Andrew lived with his dad John in the market town of Dumfries, Scotland. Their secluded country house sat perched on the edge of the River Nith, speckled by the shadows of a tree-lined country lane. Andrew was an only child, and since his parents' divorce three years ago, had been the sole carer for John who suffered from Parkinson's disease. With no close family, Andrew shared a tight bond with his dad. They spent hours playing cards by the fire, talking about cars and football and travel. Despite a rumbling desire to venture away from the confines of the Highlands, Andrew lived his life for his dad.

In autumn of 2016, Andrew had finished his shift at the local car garage and was walking home along the curling paths of the river. Shrouded in fire-coloured leaves, Andrew moved steadily until he noticed a beacon of light. A flashing blue rhythm interrupted the glistening autumnal array. Something wasn't right. Andrew jumped a wall to find an ambulance parked firmly on his driveway. His dear dad John had passed away.

In the months that followed, Andrew spiralled into a pit of confusion. Everything he lived for was gone. He didn't know who he was anymore, or what he could contribute to the world. Where did he belong if he had no family? What was his purpose if it was not to care for his dad? Andrew took residency in the local pub, drinking beer every night and staring blankly at his friends who seemed to be talking like nothing had ever happened. Desperate to avoid returning to an empty home, Andrew began taking drugs. He didn't want to feel anything. He was looking for an escape. Weeks passed and he became more reckless, throwing himself under the scrutiny of his work colleagues. Thanks to his dad, Andrew was a brilliant mechanic who knew everything there was to know about cars. But Andrew's coping mechanism was costing him his job, with only so many late mornings and mindless mistakes seeming acceptable.

On Christmas Eve, Andrew met his friends at the pub and survived yet another evening of trying to numb the pain. Dumfries families were tucked away in their cosy, festive homes, whilst Andrew entered his empty house with nothing but the lingering smell of hops and a pain in his chest. He reached his dark and dampened bedroom, stumbling through the door in a drunken state. A tear crept from his eye, but anger filled his mind. After months of denial, confusion and looking for something or someone to blame,

Andrew stared at himself in the mirror. He stared hard at his own face, piercing his fear with reality. For years he had been living his life for someone else. He had done it for love, yes, but the routine had caused his identity to become blurred. He didn't really know who he was anymore. And now he felt abandoned and confused, with no grasp of control or understanding of why. Finally, in a moment of pure emotion, Andrew was transformed by the realisation that through his grief and despair, pain and anxiety, the answer he was searching for had been in front of him all along. On January 2nd, Andrew applied to a mechanical engineering course and impressed the tutors with his passion for the subject. They welcomed him onto their programme and within a few weeks he became their top performer. Finally, with a little bit of soul searching, Andrew was able to pursue a life he loved.

The trauma trigger is unique in comparison to all other triggers mentioned previously. This trigger has the potential to happen suddenly with no prior warning signs, whereas the others often gradually occur over time. It is usually much bigger and more catastrophic. When facing trauma, we are much more susceptible to making fleeting, irrational decisions that could hugely impact our existence and well-being. However, as with all other QLC triggers, trauma does invite us to stop and question ourselves on a very deep level. Despite the obvious emotional pain we may feel as a result of trauma, we have to understand that devastating opportunities do not mean that our lives are over. In fact, they can be invitations for us to seriously focus on the value of living and the precious nature of time. Trauma encourages us to adapt to our newly assigned path. Instead of cowering in a corner – wondering 'why me?' – we should try to face the fear and ask 'what next?'

CHAPTER TWO – TAKEAWAYS

- Human beings have the capability of using reason and language to pursue meaningful and rational endeavours, allowing us to create our own life goals.
- We often fail to actively reinvent our goals as context changes, leaving us susceptible to disappointment.
- The moments of realisation and subsequent QLC are triggered by burnout, dissatisfaction, comparisons or trauma.
- Accepting that these triggers are inevitable, and learning to deal with them, will equip us with the adaptability we need to survive a QLC.

CHAPTER THREE

In Chapters One and Two, we identified that a QLC occurs when you perform a spot check on your life and feel that you are not quite where you want to be at that particular age or moment. The trigger for the spot check can vary and may involve burnout, dissatisfaction, comparing yourself to others or trauma. The QLC involves being confused about your life purpose and feeling unclear about what will make you happy. Spending too much time online is a significant cause of anxiety and distracts you from digging deeper to understand what will truly make you happy and give your life purpose. Sometimes, you may feel that you have already identified your purpose but you still experience a QLC. This could be because your purpose needs to change, or you identified the wrong purpose and life is trying to put you on a new path. Ultimately, the reason for a QLC is because life is telling you that you need to pay attention to yourself and make a change. The best part about all of this is that change is coming and you are in complete control.

I am about to talk you through my tried and tested steps of how to survive a QLC. I am really excited to share all of this with you. But first, I want to make sure that your mindset is in the right place. There will be some sceptics reading this book – people who have tried to make changes but feel that they are a constant victim of the bullshit that life has to offer. I'm sure that they will feel very doubtful about the prospect of this book being their magical key to happiness. What you need to know is that there is no way to stop life from challenging you. But it is possible to redefine your goals, control your mindset and get better at coping with problems. As a result of this process, you will reduce confusion and anxiety, which will allow you to live happily. Regardless of how many times you have been knocked down in the past, you *can* and *will* reach success if you want to. You have to spend time looking inward so that you can discover what happiness is to you. You must then pursue this vision with every inch of determination in your body. As a result, your life will be enriched with experiences that truly mean something, rather than being full of routine, social media slavery or general pointlessness. Bear in mind that this is not a fixed procedure (as I will discuss in the final chapter), and you will most likely need to repeat the process numerous times throughout your life. Most importantly, controlling your mindset is integral to surviving your QLC, and that is exactly where we will begin.

Firstly, let's have a look at how habits work. Habits often dictate our behaviour, so if we can control our habits, we can surely control our mindset. Generally speaking, with all formed habits, there is a *cue* (something that tells your brain to act). This then triggers a *routine*, which could be a physical movement, a feeling or emotion. Finally, there is a *reward*, which will be the deciding factor for whether or not your brain will repeat the 'habit' in the future.[16] An example of this cycle could be the social recognition that occurs from our use of social media, which we have already discussed. Firstly, the *cue* is the red notification that pops up on the home screen of your mobile phone. Secondly, the *routine* is the physical pressing of buttons which allows you to open the app. Finally, the *reward* is the dopamine experience that results from finding that someone has 'liked' your recent post. When practising this routine several times, it becomes a habit and we become addicted. Another example of behavioural conditioning is the 'Pavlov's Dogs' theory, a psychology experiment conducted by Ivan Pavlov in 1889. In the experiment, Pavlov gave a dog some food and simultaneously rang a bell (cue). The dog would salivate at the sight of the food (routine) and then enjoy eating his meal (reward). After repeating this process numerous times, the dog became classically conditioned to salivate when hearing the sound of a bell, even if the food was not present.[17] In essence, the dog learned a new behaviour/formed a new habit, and you can too.

What is most interesting is that it is possible for us to learn new behaviour at any age and stage or our life. For example, most of us learned the social media habit cycle as teenagers or young adults. This, therefore, means that it is also possible to *change* our behaviour at any age and stage of our life, and this is exactly what we need to do when we enter a QLC. And if you still need convincing after all that science, read *How to Live on Twenty-Four Hours a Day* by Arnold Bennett. Who can argue with a Nobel Prize-winning author who writes very confidently that "mind control is the first element of a full existence…"?[18] I will discuss Bennett's writing a bit more later on, but for now, start to believe that you can change your thoughts and control your own mind. When you arrive in that headspace, you can really start surviving a QLC.

THE PURPOSE PYRAMID

Let's look at your life as a pyramid.

You'll notice that *purpose* is sitting right at the top of the pyramid, but the four steps beneath it are currently blank. I want you to reach purpose because this will cure your QLC, but you cannot reach the top of your pyramid without using the four missing steps. At various points in your life, these steps will sit robustly in their correct place and you will find it relatively easy to stay perched right at the top. At the minute, however, your pyramid's steps have become abstract or completely invisible. This explains why you currently feel such a loss of clarity with who you are and what your life journey is.

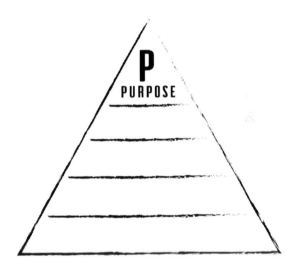

As we acknowledged in the previous chapter, your problems have been caused by life curveballs and now you need to spend some time looking inward to start rebuilding those steps. It is worth noting that steps cannot be missed. Each layer of the pyramid is crucial to navigating your way to the top. You can't rebuild step two without paying attention to the foundation of step one. It is also worth noting that each step has a common requirement for continued progression. This requirement is something that many people talk about, but not many people genuinely have. It is a requirement that you may feel will come as a reward for reaching your purpose, but in fact it cannot and will not ever be gifted to you. The requirement is *self-worth*, and it will glue your pyramid together from foundation to peak. We will discuss this in more detail first.

SELF-WORTH

There's a voice inside your head. You know what I'm talking about. It feels like it belongs to you, but *boy* does it have a mind of its own. You know when you're trying to get to sleep, but all you can hear is that voice talking, talking, talking, TALKING?

'That project at work is a shit-show. How am I going to salvage it?! And what was Claire talking about in the catch-up meeting today? Shit. I forgot to give her my handover notes like I said I would. I hope she's not angry tomorrow. Do I even have anything to wear tomorrow? I've worn that blue shirt two days in a row… not sure if anyone noticed. Hope Greg didn't notice. Will he ever actually ask me out? It's been three weeks of desk flirting and he's not even asked me out! Am I imagining that he fancies me? Oh God. What if I'm imagining that he fancies me? Well, that's embarrassing. Shit. I haven't set my alarm.'

Ok, you get the idea.

The voice particularly likes to come out to play at night, when you tuck yourself into bed. But when you pay attention, it's there all the time, slowly rambling on to you in the background. When you walk down the street, go to the supermarket, sit at family meals or visit your friends, there's a constant life narration happening, courtesy of your own little inner voice. Although the inner voice can be a bit annoying sometimes, especially when you are trying to sleep, the real trouble arises when your inner voice is in a bad mood. See, it has the habit of turning on the person closest to it. That person is you.

'You look dreadful today. Look at the bags under your eyes. Everyone in the meeting today will think you look tired. They won't even listen to a word you are saying because of how terrible you look. And if they do listen to what you are saying, you are completely unprepared so they will laugh at how much of a fraudster you are. You will never get that promotion. Amy is much better at the job than you.'

We would all probably agree that our inner voice is very influential of our mood. It has the incredible power of saying exactly what it wants, sometimes to the point of completely ruining our day. But why can't we control it like we can control our external voice?

I've sat in many meetings where my inner voice has said some pretty sassy things about some of my colleagues, but luckily I am in complete control of my external voice so those conversations never saw the light of day. *Cue influx of texts from angry work colleagues*. The thing is, we DO have control of our inner voice. Research has proven that our inner speech is a form of internalised vocalisation that uses similar brain mechanisms as the ones activated when we actually speak out loud.[19] Although inner speech is incredibly complicated in its own right, we do have the power to control it.

Let's start right now. Look away from the pages of this book, and in your head slowly say the words, *hairy hippopotamus* three times.

Ok, let's try something else. Look away from the pages of this book, and in your head tell yourself how *f*cking awesome you are*.

Our inner voice simply narrates what it sees at face value on a daily basis. You see the postman and your inner voice tells you, 'there's the postman!' When you look at yourself, especially during a QLC, your inner voice will narrate some particularly negative and emotionally crippling things. You need to control what your inner voice tells you, just like you did with hairy hippopotamus and the fact that you are f*cking awesome. When you look in the mirror, apply for a job, plan your career change, go on a date or spend time relaxing, you need to interrupt the dictatorship of your inner voice and tell yourself all the positive things that you deserve to hear in order to build your self-worth.

Self-worth: *the sense of one's own value or worth as a person.*[20]

Self-worth is often confused with self-esteem, but they are different. Self-esteem focusses on measuring ourselves based on external actions, whereas self-worth is much more of an intrinsic value. How do you really *feel* about yourself? If the answer to that question is negative, and I'm sure 90 percent of the population would say it is, then you have some work to do. The journey to surviving a QLC is based entirely on looking inward using self-reflection in order to identify what we want and how to get there. So, continually convincing ourselves that we are an awesome person and totally worthy of happiness is crucial to helping us complete the following steps. Bad self-worth is going to hold you back, my friend. Get. Rid. Of. It.

STEP ONE – WORK

Ready to start surviving this QLC? Let's get started!

Every pyramid needs a foundation, and your foundation is work. The mistake that many people make is treating work as a chore. Although work is a requirement for obtaining financial stability, the tasks within the job itself are a huge reason why we feel purpose.

In Ancient Greek philosophy, Aristotle explored the definition of happiness (something he called Eudaimonia) and decided that man's function is what distinguishes him from all other beings. Aristotle believed that happiness is felt when a man's function, or activity in which he specialises in, is performed well. This is the reason why it is crucial that your outlook on work is not solely to earn money, but instead to form part of your function as a human being. You may prefer to call your job your *craft*, or your *profession*. The best way to view your job is as an opportunity for you to become an expert in your chosen field; someone that others can approach for knowledge on a particular subject.

When you are recognised and praised by other people for your expertise, you will feel that you are contributing something of value and significance to the world, and in turn your self-worth will rapidly grow. As mentioned, self-worth is integral to help solidify each individual layer of your pyramid. You need an abundance of self-worth to truly feel that you can and will reach happiness. It is an element that will become stronger in time and with age, practise and experience, but to begin with, focus on achieving a happy work situation. Work forms the foundation of your pyramid, and the rewards you receive from this function are the reason why you should always strive to view your job as a positively beneficial activity.

The majority of millennials feel that trying to find a job or career that they are passionate about is the number one cause for their QLC. Fifty-four percent feel frustrated by their career options, and 49 percent feel that they are not earning as much as they thought they would be at their age.[21] This research tells us that our generation has a huge passion for work, so much so that the pressure we put on ourselves to find job utopia is having a serious effect on our collective well-being. To reiterate, understanding the importance of work is not necessarily the cause of a QLC; instead, it is more to do with the work expectations that we place on ourselves.

I always feel that parents and grandparents of millennials are very confused about the meltdowns we often have about work.

For war-time workers, the concept of being able to endlessly pick and choose what to study and what industry to work in seems completely alien. It's the ultimate 'first-world problem' in their eyes, and understandably so. My Grandma told me about how she always dreamt of being a florist. In reality, her job was to support the man of the house. As a child, she would wash and fold her dad's uniform in preparation for his return to war. In later years, she would look after her own children while Grandad worked in the pit. She tells us how Grandad would earn £23 a week, spend £3 on the mortgage, £3 on bills and give her £6 for housekeeping. They could only afford romantic date nights on special occasions, like Grandma's birthday and their wedding anniversary. One week, my Grandma asked Grandad if she could have a lipstick and some new stockings. Unable to scrape the pennies, he innocently answered, "Are you able to have the lipstick this week, and the stockings next week, my love?" It's stories like these that often make me wonder how I could ever expect my Grandma to understand why I have explored so many different jobs over the years, especially when one big ASOS order allows me to have as many lipsticks, stockings and inflatable avocados that I can physically cram into my bedroom. Sometimes I feel like the female version of Leonardo Di-Caprio in *Catch Me If You Can*. Airline pilot one week, doctor the next. (Ok, so I've never been a pilot or doctor, but there's still time.) Our career choice paralysis is barely on the same page of problems that my Grandma encountered in her 20s. In fact, I've noticed that she has altogether stopped asking me how work is when I go to visit her. Bless her soul, I think she is completely lost with what I spend my days doing. And to be quite frank, every now and then, I feel completely lost with what I spend my days doing. As do the majority of QLC sufferers right now. What's most important is acknowledging that work is an opportunity to develop our function and learn our self-worth. It's also important that we appreciate the vast array of career choices we are lucky to have, unlike so many of our predecessors. It upsets me to think that my dear Grandma hasn't been able to live her professional floristry dream. But what does make me smile is that she never gave up on her passion. Every Christmas she creates a special Christmas candle flower arrangement for our dinner table. It's the most heart-warming gift we ever receive.

One of my favourite stories of work success comes from a man named Howard Schultz. Howard grew up in New York City in a working-class Jewish family. His mother was a receptionist, and his father was a driver and factory worker. When Howard was only seven years old, his father broke his ankle and was unable to work. The family had no source of income. Somewhat moved by the distressing vision of his father left helplessly laying on the couch with his leg in a cast, Howard pursued his high school sports passion and earned a scholarship to Northern Michigan University. He became the first college graduate of his family. With a festering sense of ambition, Howard got his first graduate job on a sales training program at Xerox where he learned to cold-call and pitch. He then progressed to a company called Hammarplast, working hard through the ranks until he became vice president and general manager of Perstorp. Despite what most may deem to be a robustly successful career, Howard secretly knew he was not truly fulfilled by his job. So he continued to search.

Hammarplast owned a small coffee shop chain with four stores in Seattle. One day, when the shops ordered an unusually large amount of coffee, Howard went to investigate. On arrival, the owners of the coffee chain greeted Howard and shared their passion for their gourmet coffee niche. Howard experienced something he had never felt before – an epiphany of sorts. The people who worked there were really happy, and their happiness had an undeniable impact on the success of their business. This was the very feeling Howard had been missing in his career, and he wasn't prepared to let it go. As a result of his trip, Howard gave up his fancy job with a sterling salary and moved across the country to Seattle to work for the small coffee chain. Years later, through hard work and dedication, he became the company's CEO. The company I am talking about is Starbucks.[22]

Take the time to think about your job. Overall, do you enjoy it? Do you feel valued? Do you feel challenged? Do you earn enough? If your immediate thoughts are negative, this step could be damaged and prevent you from climbing to reach your purpose. Remember that you can't skip a step, so if you are struggling to feel that your pyramid's foundation is strong and reliable, then it urgently requires some attention. Try to pinpoint what parts of your job you dislike. Is it the people you work with? Perhaps your boss is causing you serious stress? Or is it the work itself that feels deeply unsatisfying, too difficult or too easy? Is the commute completely exhausting you? Or are the hours not giving you enough time to enjoy other aspects of your life?

Pick apart every aspect of your job until you can clearly identify what you don't enjoy. Make a list. Hopefully, then, you should start to understand if there are severe problems that need solving. It could be that your problems are short term; for example, you are working on a difficult project that will eventually end or you are working in a team with a frustrating colleague that you could attempt to speak to and find common ground. In these scenarios, you should act to change and improve that particular situation. However, if you have been feeling down for several months or longer, then the problem is most likely permanent and you should probably consider changing your job.

According to global studies, 53 percent of Americans are currently unhappy at work and 79 percent of people who quit their jobs cite 'lack of appreciation' as their reason for leaving.[23] It's concerning to see that a large number of employees are not taking the time to recognise the knock-on effect that their unhappiness in the workplace can have on the rest of their well-being. It is also worth emphasising the importance of establishing yourself within a team that will offer you the appreciation you deserve for your efforts. I am absolutely not suggesting that when things get a little difficult, you quit. Some of my greatest achievements have been the result of practising perseverance, patience and resilience through difficult work situations. But what I do suggest is that if you are feeling lost in a QLC, your job could be the root cause, and if it is, you simply need to understand that the world is full of opportunities and you should not feel trapped or isolated. There are always other options.

On the flip side, you may be unemployed. Perhaps you have been made redundant or have finished studying and can't seem to secure a graduate job. Maybe you took a career break, had health issues, had a baby or have been travelling for a while. Whether your unemployment is self-initiated or not, it could be a huge contributing factor to the reason why you are experiencing a QLC. This also reinforces the notion that work is not just about earning money. Work is a way to develop skills and feel a strong sense of self-worth. There is no doubt that during a time of unemployment, you may begin to lose who you are as a person and forget what your life purpose is. Those feelings of doubt and uncertainty have forced the foundation of your pyramid to be removed.

The good news here is that you now understand the connection between your overwhelming feelings of QLC and the need to have a job. With this in mind, you can take appropriate action to rebuild this primary step. You may start a side hustle like making and selling jewellery, or blogging about a subject that you love. Or maybe you will delve into the wonderful world of charity work, allowing you to improve the lives of other people as well as reinstating your own self-worth. If you are actively looking for a new job but no matter how many applications you send no one seems to want to employ you (we've all been there), it could be time to re-strategise. Are there any courses you could go on to improve your skillset so that you have additional selling points on your CV? Maybe you need to follow up on more of your applications with gentle and friendly phone calls. I am a firm believer in 'it's not what you know, but who you know', so have a think about your friend and family network. Is there anyone that can put you in touch with their contacts who work in your field of interest? And finally, we live in a world of amazing connectedness.

Have you thought about utilising a web presence more? I recently saw someone who had recorded a video CV and uploaded it to LinkedIn to better showcase their personality. It got a ridiculous number of shares and landed the guy a brilliant job. It is your personality and passion that employers are really looking for, so think outside of the box, and don't be afraid to show yourself off.

While this is not a career guidance book, I hope that you now feel a fresh sense of rationalisation and the encouragement you need to act upon any feelings of doubt and dissatisfaction that you may be experiencing at work. I hope that you are also now beginning to feel more motivated and inspired to survive your QLC. It boils down to being able to pull apart the various causes of your unhappiness and then directly tackle those problems one by one.

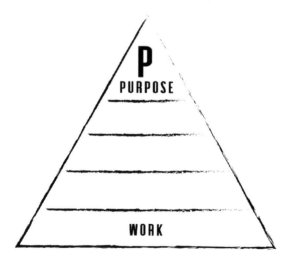

STEP TWO – LEISURE

Once you have established a rhythm of work that fulfils you, you can move on to the next step of your pyramid. Leisure is essential to balance with work so that our brains remain healthy. In history, Greek tragedian Euripides (480-406 BC) explored concepts of individuals and their inner conflicts. In his play, *The Bacchae*, a prophet named Tiresias tells King Pentheus that human beings are subject to two forces: bread and wine. Bread represents the controlled, logical mind (work), and wine represents a free, loss of mind (play). The king ignores Tiresias' wisdom to keep these elements equally balanced and falls victim to the complete temptation of Dionysius, god of wine. Through allowing himself to become lured by vain and boastful behaviour, King Pentheus' fate results in him being brutally torn apart by his own mother.[24] A little dramatic, it may seem. I'm sure you won't be pulled apart by your mother any time soon. But the concept makes sense both philosophically and psychologically. Too much control is unhealthy. Too much freedom is unhealthy. The tip of the scales could swing in either direction and in order to avoid a dramatic internal conflict, such as a QLC, we have to make sure that we take care when walking the tightrope of life.

In contrast to the Greek tragedy, though, we live in a world that seems to fixate on an all-work-and-no-play philosophy. Sure, we can often be tempted to do things we know we shouldn't, but it could be argued that our biggest battle is allocating enough time to relaxing. A lot of employees are pressurised into arriving to work early and staying late at night in order to be deemed a valuable and successful team member. I've lost count of how many colleagues I've witnessed get promotions based on hours spent in the office rather than on the quality of their work. Ring any bells? I've always tried to avoid jobs that advertise *'applicant must expect to work some evenings and weekends'*. It's not that I don't like to pull my weight; it's that I believe in working smartly and not selling my soul to the devil. Sure, I have been in situations where legging it from the office at 5.30pm would be work suicide. I completely understand that sometimes deadlines have to be met and a few extra hours need to be completed. I take great pride in my work, so I am occasionally more than happy to do that. However, I believe that the decision for me to work extra hours in order to benefit the company should be made between myself and my employer on a project-by-project basis, rather than my employer making the immediate assumption that my position in the workplace means that my hours are forever at their disposal. Before I continue, I will caveat that I am speaking from experience as an office worker and I am aware that this principle may not work for everyone. For instance, those that work in the emergency services don't have the luxury of laying their own work-hour law down, but they should (perhaps more than anyone!) make sure that they fully utilise the time that they do have for leisure, and ensure they use this free time wisely. Thus, we return to our original concept of balance.

I must highlight here that by 'leisure' I do not mean going out on a Friday night to get so drunk that your weekend is spent admiring the insides of a toilet (I'm not trying to be the fun police, but we all know that hangovers in your 20s get substantially harder). Leisure is about indulging in activities that engage your mind, body and soul. Leisure is essentially 'play time', but it needs to be savvy. Many people would automatically opt for adrenaline-pumping and exciting activities, which are fun and great, but too much of these (alongside work) can cause burnout. To be smart, you need to dedicate time to appreciate the simplest moments in life – the ones that allow you to truly relax. So, what do you love to do outside of work? Below are some of my go-to activities for leisure:

• Wake up on a Saturday morning and read books in bed
• Go for a walk to somewhere I've never been before
• Eat incredible food at a nice restaurant with friends
• Plan a trip or holiday
• Exercise
• Write
• Go to a concert or gig

You get the idea. It's all pretty normal stuff, right? Don't get me wrong, I have done some incredible things on my travels, like helicopter rides into the Grand Canyon and quad biking through Icelandic mountains. But these extravagant activities are not daily occurrences that allow me to relax. Sure enough, holidays, travelling and other exciting activities deliver the ultimate character-building moments and experiences that are integral to us forming well-rounded opinions on life and culture, but sometimes they can distract us from learning to enjoy mundane things that we so often take for granted and cloud our brain with dopamine and adrenaline. We then become unfamiliar with enjoying quieter moments of peace and reflection and, in turn, find it even more challenging to navigate unavoidable moments of chaos and stress. The aim of the leisure step in our Purpose Pyramid is to establish a strong, comfortable daily mindset that balances our work foundation. By identifying and then pursuing subtle, relaxing leisurely activities (and gradually seeing the health benefits), we are training our brains to cope with both extremes of crazy and calm.

For added reassurance, many scientific studies have shown that including leisure in our lifestyle can reduce the risk of illness and disease. French studies have shown that people who regularly indulge in a diverse range of leisurely activities (travelling, odd jobs, knitting) all lower their risk of dementia, and New York City studies have shown that people who regularly enjoy activities such as reading, board games, music and dancing have a reduced risk of dementia by 38 percent.[25] These findings are quite fantastic and should empower us with the knowledge that enjoying ourselves outside of work is important and healthy.

Perhaps this is why meditation and yoga are two of the most popular leisure activities of recent years. People have tried and witnessed the incredibly powerful impact of taking time out of their hectic working lives to stop, breathe and enjoy doing... nothing! But your leisure time doesn't have to be conventional. As I've listed above, your leisure time can and should be completely personal to you.

Why don't you start right now? Take a moment to stop and think about the little moments in life that bring you joy. Nothing flashy or expensive. Let go of your iPhone and put your purse away. I'm thinking more along the lines of the sound of torrential rain hitting your window on a cosy Sunday morning. Or the smell of fresh coffee. Or the feeling of the sun warming your face as you walk through country lanes in the summer. You know, the moments that actually remind you that you are alive. Try it for a few minutes.

Struggling to concentrate? It's ok. There will always be busy and stressful thoughts whirling around your head, refusing to leave you alone. This is why I asked you to think about a *hairy hippopotamus* earlier. Slowing your pace, controlling your thoughts and relaxing is difficult, but if you practice doing all of these things, you will really begin to enjoy your life.

Referring back to Arnold Bennett's *How to Live on Twenty-Four Hours a Day*, the nature of our leisure time should include an element of self-reflection.[26] Barely any of us actually know ourselves. We spend more time trying to shave our armpits carefully than taking care of our own well-being. Most people are petrified to open a can of worms and examine the insides of their own crazy brain, but the benefits of facing your thoughts head-on are invaluable. Nothing good comes from burying your head in the sand. But everything good can come from solving personal problems.

In a nutshell, don't let the pressure of work and other life stresses defer you from enjoying some quality 'you' time. Your health depends on it. Just as work is a requirement in order to get paid and find your function, leisure is a requirement in order to nurture your well-being and discover more about yourself. These elements run in sync with each other to feed your life with all the nutritional basics.

Task for today: Find something ordinary that calms you. Revisit this experience daily to remind you that happiness can be found in the simplest of places.

STEP THREE – SKILL

I've hinted previously that it is possible to change our behaviour and learn new habits. The cure for a QLC lies within our own ability to reinstate control of our thoughts and mindset. This is all scientifically possible, as we will begin to see when discussing the third step of the Purpose Pyramid: skill.

The human brain is what sets us apart from any other species. As an overview, our brains are made up of billions of neurons which create electrical signals that last for a thousandth of a second. Active neurons form these electrical connections with other cells to create a 'synapse', which in turn triggers the release of chemical messengers called 'transmitters'. This incredible network of activity is happening within numerous regions of our brain, each one dedicated to performing different mental functions. A child's brain has twice as many synapses as an adult's, which is why children are often much more able to learn new things, such as languages (provided that their neural connections are continually reinforced), and why adults may sometimes find learning more difficult. In theory, when we reach our 20s our brain has hit its peak performance, and by our late 20s it begins to slow down completely. It loses volume, the cortex becomes thinner and neurons don't fire as quickly. By the time we turn 60, our brain begins to shrink completely.[27]

That's the scary stuff out of the way. Now on to the magic.

For years, people have believed that the human brain runs as a fixed entity. It has been assumed that when we reach adulthood, the hardwiring of our brain is unchangeable. This is often how we, as individuals, feel throughout our lives. If new opportunities or challenges feel too difficult to us, we assume that we are at the peak of our performance and give up. But many neuroscientists have been determined to prove that this is not the case.

In a ground-breaking early '90s experiment, Alvaro Pascual-Leone exposed three groups of adult volunteers to a piano. Group One was asked to stare at the piano. Group Two learnt to play some simple piano exercises and Group Three subjects were asked to *imagine* they were playing the piano but not touch it. During brain scans, the participants in Groups Two and Three astonishingly reported almost identical changes in brain activity. The part of the brain of participants who were physically playing the piano exercises was also active for participants who were merely *thinking* about playing the exercises. The neurological explanation for this is that we have the power to grow our network of neurons and increase their potential of establishing more connections just by *thinking* about a given task.[28] Physically practising the new skill over a period of time will undoubtedly mean that we become much better at it. But in terms of being able to sustain and even improve our brain power, regularly exercising our thoughts alone will suffice.

Giving our brain regular workouts will encourage its plasticity. As weightlifting in the gym builds muscle, brain stimulation builds neural connections. If we neglect learning new skills and waste our spare time scrolling through social media feeds, our brain will coast on autopilot and rapidly decline as we age. But when we feed our brain with new information (challenge it a little), it responds positively by creating new connections. Quite astonishingly, it grows. The benefits of this, aside from reducing risks of illness, are that our skills improve, our work prospects increase and our self-worth flourishes. For this part of the Purpose Pyramid, the transformation of self-worth is paramount. We already have our work foundation and dedicated leisure time, but through striving to learn more and be better, we will undoubtedly look at ourselves with a strong sense of pride and achievement. Through dedication and resilience, we will notice that we are getting better at tackling challenges, our brain feels active and healthy and our attitude towards life is much more positive.

Try and think about what sort of skills you already have and what new things you'd like to try. If you aren't sure where to begin, speak to close friends and family. Perhaps your best friend crochets, your brother plays the guitar and your flatmate collects comics. What better way to learn something new than by spending some quality time with people you love to hang out with? For a more convenient approach, online learning can be a great option. We all know that YouTube has tutorial videos on just about every topic known to mankind, but FutureLearn.com also provides hours and hours of free online courses in a range of professional subjects. If you have a busy working lifestyle, try listening to some specialist podcasts while commuting. Even just hearing experts talking about a particular subject can gradually educate you on something new. Another method I like to use to learn new skills is attending talks, courses or tradeshows. Eventbrite, Funzing and Meetup.com are all excellent organisations that offer some free and reasonably priced events that give you an insight into a diverse range of subjects. The world really is your oyster!

I recently got asked to write a Q&A with a jazz band for a magazine feature. I knew I wanted to do a great job, but wow, my knowledge of jazz is limited. To practice what I preach, I spent 24 hours fully immersing myself into a world of jazz. I researched the history of jazz, watched YouTube videos about key jazz pioneers, watched a few jazz-themed films and wrote the whole article with jazz music playing in the background. I loved it, the magazine loved the article and as a bonus, I now know the difference between Dixieland, Bebop and Modal.

At first, you might feel completely disinterested or intimidated by the subject you choose to tap into, but learning and developing new skills will inevitably feel challenging. It just means it's working.

After a few hours of engagement, you may decide to give up and move on to something else. This is ok! You have most likely learnt something new from the activity and have given your brain a mini workout in the process. The realisation that you hate crochet, are really bad at the guitar or feel completely bored by comics helps you learn about yourself, at the very least. But sometimes it is wise to push past the initial feeling of boredom or defeat because there is no better feeling than that of accomplishment. If you can persist with a new skill, and get even slightly better at it, you will feel an overwhelming surge of pride. Your neural networks will grow and your purpose will become more defined.

STEP FOUR – GIVING

You are lying in a hospital bed, strapped to a life support machine and surrounded by your family. You've lived a full and healthy life, with plentiful opportunities. You are content that your time has come because you wouldn't change a thing about the road that led you there. Through the crowd of gathering relatives, the youngest of them bounces over to you. Surrounded with a shield of innocence, spreading an aura of hope and glee, your curious little grandchild asks you a question. It will be the final question that you have the pleasure of answering while you remain alive in this world. It is the question that you wished you would have asked yourself towards the start of your journey, but one that you can easily answer at the end.

"How will the world remember you?"

There are countless differences between each of us as human beings on this planet, but two things will always remain the same: we are born, and we will die. Think about some of the legends who have walked the planet Earth: Nelson Mandela, William Shakespeare, Winston Churchill, Charles Darwin, Plato, Eleanor Roosevelt, Albert Einstein, Martin Luther King Jr., Rosa Parks, Marie Curie, Mother Teresa, Bill Gates, Steve Jobs, Pablo Picasso, to name just a few. Although it is easy to feel worlds apart from these highly influential people and what they have powerfully contributed to our lives, we should always remember that we too can create a life of value. Value not only for ourselves but for those who follow us. When we walk this earth, we leave a trail of footprints behind. The path that these footprints take is entirely within our control.

This is not to say that we should all act like heroes. It is also not to say that we should feel inadequate or like we have failed if we are not stopping world wars, inventing computer systems or challenging racial discrimination. The point is that people from all walks of life have added huge value to our world by deciding what is important to them and pursuing it. Each of the names listed above, and so many more that I would love to mention, have changed the lives of billions of people by contributing their own magical moments of art, music, science, business, politics and health. No matter how big or small the contribution, it exists, and will always exist as their legacy. Often, during times of confusion and lost identity, we need to take a moment to ask ourselves the question, *'How do I want to be remembered?'* and decide if the footsteps we are currently walking are heading in the right direction. If they are not, it is never too late to make the change.

It is true that by fulfilling the previous three steps of the Purpose Pyramid (work, leisure and skill) you may feel that you have explored every internal avenue possible and as a result found your purpose and survived your QLC. Hurrah! With those three elements combined, your self-worth, wealth and joy will inevitably skyrocket, but there will be limitations to your overall success without considering what your contribution to the world is. Countless research has suggested that it is human nature to feel psychologically rewarded by giving or helping others. The term 'warm glow'[29] is often used to describe the sense of personal satisfaction we encounter when giving. This is a slightly more selfish feeling than altruism, as warm glow involves a degree of self-interest (e.g. How does giving this gift make me feel?). By no means, though, does that emotional exchange disregard the benefit of giving, and if it is a driving force to enthuse us to give more often, then it is worthy of being recognised.

In the 2006-2008 Gallup World Poll, researchers surveyed over 200,000 participants across 120 countries and found a positive relationship between personal well-being and the act of spending money on others.[30] There are countless other studies that have also reported similar findings, despite the participants' age, culture, gender or wealth. This widespread phenomenon reinstates that in order to feel truly accomplished as a human being, we must feed our need to act charitably. To live a life of greed and selfishness will mean that we can never experience the highest peaks of emotional fulfilment. In what way you decide to give something to the world is entirely up to you. We are not talking about literal financial fundraising for charity (although everyone should do this at some stage in their lives). We are trying to identify a bigger and more personal method of giving. One that acts as an extension of you. One that you will be able to put your own spin on. One that will allow you to reach your purpose and cure your QLC. But most importantly, one that will help others. What is your gift to the world?

And there we have it. Those are the four steps that form the Purpose Pyramid.

Each one, in turn, will help you think seriously about your intrinsic values so that you are able to identify whether or not you are currently on the right path. Perhaps your path feels right, but there are a few minor problems that have caused you to enter a QLC. After working through the Purpose Pyramid, you are now able to check individual problems off your list and continue doing a great job of life. If studying the Purpose Pyramid has caused you to feel overwhelmed at how unhappy you are with so many of these elements, don't worry! By simply reading and thinking about the process required to get you back on track, you are already heading in a fabulous new direction. Take the time to work through each layer of the pyramid until you reach the top. It may take days, but it could also take years. The beauty of this structure is that you will begin to feel successful right from the very beginning. Once you have improved your work foundation, your mood will lift, the entire process will get easier and eventually you will snowball through your problems in an exciting new direction.

Excited? Me too! But before you get started with painting your new life picture, there are a few things you need to bear in mind. Let's enter the final chapter to see what these things are.

CHAPTER THREE — TAKEAWAYS

- Finding your purpose is the key to surviving your QLC.

- Solidifying elements of work, leisure, skill and giving are all required to reach your purpose.

- You must feel an abundance of self-worth in order to confidently reach happiness.

- Your purpose can change as you progress through life.

- Change is a positive entity.

CHAPTER FOUR

BE MORE BUSINESS

Loon. Makani. Wing.

These are the names of three radical projects started by Google in their elusive 'X' lab. Using 'Moonshot Thinking', Google continually invests an incredible amount of time and money in allowing staff to explore wild concepts that merge technology and science fiction. A lot of their work constitutes zero percent of Google's revenue, yet they continue to plough significant resources into trialling various crazy ideas. They believe in the concept of playful thinking in order to strike genius with inventions that will improve our lives 10 times over. And if they continue to dream up the most playful ideas imaginable, at some point one of those dreams is *really* going to take off, undoubtedly changing the way we live in this world. The self-driving car, for example, is almost on its way. But for now, Google will keep adapting and changing the structure of their projects based on what works and what doesn't work until the stars align.[31]There must be something massively liberating about being able to vocalise your most daring ideas without the fear of being ridiculed or rejected. What might happen if we were to introduce a little bit of 'Moonshot Thinking' into our own self-development?

Another example of this flexible approach to reaching success comes from the founders of Flickr, a well-known image- and video-hosting website with 87 million registered members. Caterina Fake and Stewart Butterfield were not photography experts and didn't set out to create Flickr as their super-successful prize business. The founders originally created an online game called Game Neverending in 2002, a concept which would allow hundreds of players to be involved at the same time. To keep attracting new members, Caterina and Stewart worked with a beta mindset and continually introduced new features to the game, such as instant messaging and social groups. What they didn't anticipate was that their small photo-sharing add-on would eventually become more popular than the game itself. Instead of holding on to their original passion project, Caterina and Stewart decided to run entirely with the photo-sharing platform, leaving Game Neverending behind and forming Flickr.[32] You know what else started as a game? Facebook. Mark Zuckerberg had been dabbling with the world of computers since the young age of 10, and when studying at Harvard he created a game called FaceMash. The idea was that students would vote for the hottest guys and girls on campus, but with pressure from other students and teachers, Zuckerberg quickly changed the game and formed a new concept. Thus, Facebook was born. Need I say more?[32]

In business, 'beta' refers to an experimental stage in product development where a concept is still being tested in order to generate feedback. The Google lab, Flickr and Facebook are all great examples of beta in business, but what about adopting this approach for the way we live our lives? We are living in one of the most fast-paced times in history, so a fixed approach to reaching our goals will inevitably be troublesome. To manage this, we should always have backup plans to move into if our original idea doesn't work. We often talk about a 'Plan A', which usually refers to our current life journey. 'Plan B' is usually the plan we move to if we need to change our goal or how to get there. Let's now add a 'Plan C' for extra backup. This is our complete fall-back plan, needed if absolutely everything goes to shit. For example, Plan A might be to go travelling for a few months. Plan B could be to return home and resume your regular life if after one month you don't like it or you run out of money. Plan C might be to move in with your family or friends if you find yourself jobless, moneyless and homeless (and if you have the luxury of doing so).

Most of us are able to define a sort of life plan, but often cling onto it too heavily and fail to support it with a second or third contingency option. This is where things can really begin to fall short. Not many people have drifted through life with one key goal and zero obstacles or curveballs. It is the people who aren't prepared for when things go wrong who suffer the most. We need to therefore learn to live in beta, be able to develop new plans and be ok with adapting to change if things aren't working out or if new doors open for us.

Whilst comparing our life choices to business strategies, let's not forget that 'managing expectations' creates great customer service, yet this is something we rarely do for ourselves. Imagine you are a shopkeeper and have sold your customer one single product with the promise of perfection, and that product then breaks. Imagine their disappointment and uproar when you failed to deliver your promise and you have nothing else to offer them as a replacement. Alternatively, imagine selling your customer a product with no promises of perfection, but instead giving them the ability to try a second or third product if their first pick is not satisfactory. Imagine their sense of security and satisfaction. They will leave feeling excited that they have purchased something new, but if for some reason the product doesn't make them happy, they can try one or two other products. Immediately their mindset is relaxed in the knowledge that solutions have already been prepared. They aren't leaving your shop completely blinded by false hope and excitement, but instead they are grounded with a realistic outlook and backup plans. Edging away from the concept of perfectionism and into the realms of adaptability is the key to a happy future.

You only have to glance back in time at the course of history to see how successful this sort of mindset is. The previous business examples I have mentioned particularly hone in on the way in which flexible, beta mindsets can help us to let go of stagnant or counterproductive activity and encourage positive change. Let's now think BIGGER. One of the most significant world changes occurred in Britain in the 18th century and caused 250 years of disruption to the world. The Industrial Revolution. What started as little victories soon snowballed into mass production on a worldwide scale. This change didn't happen in one smooth leap, though. The Industrial Revolution progressed through three waves: invention, application and transformation. *Invention* began with forging iron and spinning textiles in England, then moved into international *application* through Robert Fulton's steamboat and Thomas Edison's light bulb, and finally, when innovations could be mass produced around the world, *transformation* took place. Huge factories with modern medicines, cars and planes grew cities and international trade, improving the lives of everyone. This three-stage process is hugely telling for the way that change is paramount, but cannot usually occur in one bold step. If we take the industrial revolution as our guide, first we have to dream up our idea, then we have to take action, and finally we have to scale everything up to solidify the change and transform our lives completely. When things aren't going right for us, we have to remember that Rome wasn't built in a day. But as soon as we start to map out what the problems are, and ponder about our ideal outcomes, the plan of action will begin to form and we are already on our way to happiness.[33]

In the previous chapter we worked through identifying your life purpose, and step by step you will have undoubtedly formulated a plan of how to reach it. What you need to remember is that as you climb the steps of your pyramid, life will continue to throw curveballs at you. They are not necessarily directed at you, but they are going to hit you. In preparation for the occasional storm, adopting a state of beta and managing your own expectations will allow you to feel fully prepared for whatever change is about to ensue. Using the three waves of revolution, you can feel comfortable with planning the gradual process of change. Although you will sometimes feel emotionally vulnerable, all of these values will mean that once you have rebuilt your emotional strength, you can turn the page and get started with Plan B, or Plan C. Begin now to think about what path you are walking along, and which two alternative paths you could change to if the current path leads nowhere. Adopt a business approach to your own life decisions so that you can stay as prepared as possible with the ability to manage your own expectations. Understand that your first choice may not be the right choice. Be open to change when things don't feel right.

REDEFINE YOUR ATTITUDE

What happens when you work through the rational, structured processes explained in this book within the comforts of your own home, but then when you step out into the jungle, a never-ending stream of shit is launched in your direction? How do you cope with the vast minefield of troubles and woes that will undoubtedly consume you? How do you stay calm and positive when all you want to do is launch yourself off a bridge or lock yourself in a dark cupboard? It's tricky, right? Almost impossible?

Look, I'm not going to sit here and say to you that getting your life together and achieving happiness is easy. I'm also not going to promise that once you start to taste the sweetness of a happy life, it won't at any moment be pulled from beneath you. In an ideal situation, we would all achieve a solid state of mind, with clear goals and direction and an abundance of positivity to keep us focussed on where we are headed. But realistically, our external environments want to continuously challenge our logic by appearing muddled, ambiguous and chaotic. Bad life events don't exist solely to confuse us; they are merely a by-product of life running its course. Nevertheless, human brains are well equipped. Psychologists who have studied 'attitudes' defined them as essential for 'organising and handling an otherwise complex and ambiguous environment'.[34] Our attitudes are there for us to use as tools for coping with external situations that cause us to feel stressed, upset and negative.

This leads me to pose the question, in a time of crisis, what does your attitude look like? Are you a Positive Polly, Negative Nancy or just a complete martyr? Is the world out to get you? Do you see the best in everything and everyone but feel like it gets you nowhere? Think back to how you tend to react to difficult situations and use this as the base of your attitude. If you are often very pessimistic, then you need to tweak the way you respond to trouble so that you are much better equipped to cope. If you are too optimistic to the point of vulnerability, then you also need to make some adjustments to avoid getting hurt. Remember, though, one size does not fit all. The attitude you adopt for dealing with stress will be slightly different to the attitude you adopt when planning your life goals. When plotting dreams and aspirations, you can afford to be much more *idealistic*. When dealing with problems, it may pay to be more *realistic*.

There's a famous 1970s speech by Viktor Frankl featured on Ted Talks.[35] Viktor Frankl is a neurologist and psychiatrist who pioneered an approach to psychotherapy called 'Logotherapy', which (like this book) proposes that the key to happiness is in finding our meaning and purpose in life. Frankl is also a survivor of the Holocaust and used this method of therapy to comfort himself and other prisoners in the Nazi concentration camps. Having been through some of the most tragic experiences a human being could possibly encounter, Frankl captivates his audience with his strong attitude and outlook on life. The premise of this particular talk was to divulge on idealist thinking. Frankl tells us that when learning to fly a plane, he was taught to aim to land slightly further north than his destination so that despite any nervous tendency to land too soon, he would always hit the mark.

Human beings have a habit of underestimating themselves. This could be because we often default to our realistic attitude at all times instead of varying our outlook depending on the context. Frankl promotes an idealistic attitude as a means of pushing himself to achieve more. When planning our future, we should aim for our optimum so that even if we fall behind, we are still likely to land in a great place. Why limit our achievements by underestimating what we are capable of? We have to work against our human nature, which humbly assumes that we are constantly at the peak of our potential because often we are only scratching the surface. It is worth remembering, though, that an idealist attitude is one that often receives criticism for showing elements of naivety. There are other, more pragmatic thinkers in the world who constantly rely on realism and analytics to make sound and rational decisions. These types of attitudes survive perfectly well in times of stress, often living safely within the confines of their comfort zone. However, as we have touched on previously, it pays to venture outside of comfort zones and try a bit of 'Moonshot Thinking' when working to define our purpose. When it comes to deciding what we want in life, we should aim to reach our ideal outcome and then be pleasantly surprised with the subsequent results.

An idealist attitude can work perfectly well when we are merrily planning our ultimate life journey, but it is difficult to be all smiles and laughter when things turn sour. Some days we wake up feeling unexplainably low and sad, or something terrible happens during our day to take us from Positive Polly to Negative Nancy in 0.5 seconds. At this point, the expectation to remain permanently positive and upbeat is completely unrealistic. It's times like these that we could all become a little more stoic. A stoic attitude is one that does not allow a person to be controlled by the desire for pleasure or fear of pain. Stoics understand that some life events are entirely out of their control and value themselves more than material things. It goes much deeper than this in Ancient Greek philosophy, with most stoics being criticised for their lack of connection with any sort of emotion. Just to be clear, I think it is very important to show emotion, but being able to let go of negative situations that we cannot control is paramount to navigating life and surviving your QLC.

A stoic attitude: *serenity in the face of a setback.*[36]

Like anything in life, knowing *what* we should do to be happy is one thing, but understanding *how* to implement these behaviours is something completely different. Towards the start of this book, I discussed our human ability to learn and change our habits. The need for social media recognition is a formed habit, as is the salivation of Pavlov's dogs when hearing a bell ring. This principle remains the same for changing our own personal attitude towards life circumstances. We must learn to accept that bad or unfair things will happen to us through the course of our lives, as will numerous exciting and exhilarating things. Our emotions will fluctuate based on our experiences, and our attitudes will help us get through the experience. Compare attitude to the weather, for example. No matter what the forecast is, life must go on. We put up an umbrella in a rainstorm and wear sunscreen in a heatwave. It's not so bad, right? So if we can train ourselves to identify what is truly important to us, and redefine our attitude to cope with unpredictable emotions, we are much more likely to be able to write a great life story for ourselves, even in times of difficulty.

CHAPTER FOUR — TAKEAWAYS

- Use business acumen to deal with your emotions when challenge strikes.
- A realistic attitude will help you to control your emotions when stressed.
- An idealist attitude will help you reach your full potential.
- Change is a positive entity.

LAST WORDS

I know, I know. I've just thrown a LOT at you.

Don't feel overwhelmed. Let's summarise a few things.

You are here because you think you are having a quarter-life crisis. Your QLC has occurred because you performed a spot check on where you are at with your life, and the results don't seem to meet the expectations you had for this given age/moment. The spot check was potentially triggered by burnout, dissatisfaction with your routine, comparing yourself to others or a traumatic event. In order to survive your QLC, you must do some robust inward thinking with a controlled mindset so that you can identify your purpose. To help simplify this process, you can refer to your very own Purpose Pyramid. Step by step, you need to address your happiness in terms of work, leisure, skill and giving. To glue these steps together, you should make sure that you are living with an abundance of self-worth. When you have developed a plan to ensure that your life is full of each of these key elements, you will undoubtedly be on the right track to reach your purpose and survive your QLC. But before you bounce with glee and feature this book smugly on your wall of fame, remember that life will always throw curveballs at you. Adopting a business mindset and redefining your attitude will equip you with the resilience you need to cope in an ever-changing world. Remember, you are always in control and it is never too late to find happiness.

I hope that you are now feeling energised, excited and inspired to get to work and carve your brilliant new life path. I hope that you realise that this world is full of endless possibilities and you should never feel incapable or backed into a corner. At the very least, I hope that this book has reassured you in the knowledge that you are not alone. The majority of millennials are experiencing the confusion that you are experiencing; we're all just too damn proud to make a song and dance about it. Taking the time to look after yourself and decide which life path you want to pursue will help to answer a lot of your problems. Be open to change, set-backs and stepping outside of your comfort zone. And if, for some reason, your purple hair is still wilting at the idea of reaching success any time soon, here's one final story to inspire you with your journey.

Chloe is a 28-year-old digital nomad living between Mallorca, the UK and Europe. Her successful marketing business runs workshops for large corporate firms and small companies alike.

From the outside looking in, Chloe has well and truly got her life together, but as we all know, the path to success is never plain sailing.

It all began four years ago when Chloe was granted the business loan she needed to pursue her dream of self-employment. *Kerching!* Thousands of pounds hit her bank account, and for the first time in her life Chloe understood what it felt like to have money. It was the summer of 2016, and while Chloe had been burying her head in the business world for a number of years, everyone else seemed to be frolicking through fields of self-enlightenment, travelling and exploring. Chloe tried to remain focussed but her FOMO got the better of her. For one final splash of fun before she thrust herself into adulthood, Chloe treated herself to a weekend-long festival break.

In the blink of an eye, autumn had arrived, and a flashback of the entire summer ignited Chloe's wanderlusting heart. She had spent a huge chunk of her business loan on festival-hopping, and in fear of being trapped in the place that her parents had lived their entire lives, Chloe decided she needed to put her business dream on hold to go and explore. Quicker than the turn of British weather, Chloe packed up her life and booked a one-way flight to sunny Mallorca.

The next few months were a whirlwind. Chloe lived with hippies in a community house, sofa surfed and flirted with bankruptcy. She moved back to the UK to pursue her dream job as a Marketing Manager, tackle the debt that her Spanish dream had created and cope with burnout and shattered confidence. Eventually, Chloe ventured back to Mallorca in the hope that another fairy tale escape would help her find her happy place, but when faced with a workaway-gone-wrong, she was forced to make her final escape back home.

It was December, and Chloe found a quiet house sitting job on the coast. She began tapping into her own version of self-reflection, spending her time doing yoga and reading self-development books. Through rejecting any form of chaos, and secluding herself in a period of inward thinking, Chloe quickly realised that she had come full circle and her true calling had been staring her in the face: her business. She designed her own marketing and goal-setting handbook and uploaded it to her website. Within days the website had hundreds of hits, and now Chloe works with a portfolio of exciting clients, helping them to set their own goals and achieve business success.

Though Chloe is thriving and successful, she warns that sometimes it feels like her QLC is ongoing.

"Two of my friends own properties, and I just don't know how that's going to happen with me because I live very hand to mouth sometimes, and love to take on projects and take risks. Maybe that's just not my path. I want to cram as much stuff in as possible. I want life experience and learning, before it is too late."

Chloe finishes:

"I have a lot of older friends, and they say all the time, 'Well I'm 70 and I haven't worked life out yet, so how can you?'"

We are all determined to become experts at life, but what art form should we really try to master? Perhaps we should put less pressure on our need to have *everything* and focus more on enjoying our own journey. After all, doesn't the key to happiness really lie in our ability to be happy with ourselves?

AcknowleDGements

Writing this book started out as one of my bucket list goals, but before I knew it I was embarking on an incredible project that I feel truly passionate about and have learnt a great deal from.

I am ridiculously proud of myself for finishing this, but there are a few people who have helped me (more than they will ever know) along the way.

Firstly, thank you to my wonderful parents who always welcome me into their home to take refuge, hide, heal and store my millions of clothes. Your support is cherished.

Thank you to my friends who have charged me with motivation, picked me up when I'm down and championed my strength and determination. Through many meltdowns, you have shown me the light.

Thank you to Richard McMunn, an author who inspired me to self-publish this book on a free course he ran in London earlier this year.

Thank you to my dear Grandma, Andrew and Chloe Morris for allowing me to write about your amazing life stories. Please check out Chloe's website: www.pinkflamingomarketing.com, or follow her on Instagram @pinkflamingomarketing

And finally, thank you to anyone who has invested time and money into reading my work. I hope it has had a positive impact on your life in some way, and that we can stay in touch in the future.

References

INTRODUCTION

1. Sarah Young, 'More Than Half of Millennials Going Through 'Quarter-Life Crisis', Research Finds', Independent, (last updated 13th March 2018), https://www.independent.co.uk/life-style/millennials-quarter-live-crisis-half-25-35-finance-career-property-first-direct-a8253036.html

CHAPTER ONE

2. Simon Parkin, 'Has Dopamine Got Us Hooked on Tech?', The Guardian, (last updated 4th March 2018), https://www.theguardian.com/technology/2018/mar/04/has-dopamine-got-us-hooked-on-tech-facebook-apps-addiction

3. Shainna Ali, Ph.D., 'Is Social Media Making You Lonely?', Psychology Today, (last updated 5th October 2018), https://www.psychologytoday.com/intl/blog/modern-mentality/201810/is-social-media-making-you-lonely

4. Paul Dolan. Happiness By Design. Penguin Books 2015. (Page 15)

5. William Walker Atkinson. Your Mind and How to Use It: A Manual of Practical Psychology. Originally published 1911. (Page 27)

6. Anthony Storr. The Essential Jung. Selected Writings Introduced by Anthony Storr. Fontana Press 1998. (Page 21)

7. Anthony Storr. The Essential Jung. Selected Writings Introduced by Anthony Storr. Fontana Press 1998. (Page 193)

8. https://en.wikipedia.org/wiki/Existential_crisis

CHAPTER TWO

9. William Walker Atkinson. Your Mind and How to Use It: A Manual of Practical Psychology. Originally published 1911. (Page 27)

10. Moya Sarner, 'How burnout became a sinister and insidious epidemic', The Guardian, (last updated 21st February 2018), https://www.theguardian.com/society/2018/feb/21/how-burnout-became-a-sinister-and-insidious-epidemic

11. Remez Sasson, 'How Many Thoughts Does Your Mind Think in One Hour?', Success Consciousness, https://www.successconsciousness.com/blog/inner-peace/how-many-thoughts-does-your-mind-think-in-one-hour/

12. David W. Robinson. Conscience and Jung's Moral Vision: From Id to Thou. (Page 117)

13. Chris Weller, 'Bill Gates and Steve Jobs raised their kids tech-free – and it should've been a red flag', Business Insider, (last updated 10th January 2018), http://uk.businessinsider.com/screen-time-limits-bill-gates-steve-jobs-red-flag-2017-10

14. Héctor Garcia and Francesc Miralles. Ikigai: The Japanese Secret to a Long and Happy Life. Hutchinson 2017 (Page 66)

15. Pooky Knightsmith, 'New Research Finds That Facebook Use Is Linked To Depressive Symptoms', Lifehack, https://www.lifehack.org/articles/communication/new-research-finds-that-facebook-use-linked-depressive-symptoms.html

CHAPTER THREE

16. Charles Duhigg. The Power Of Habit. Random House Books 2013. (Page 19)

17. Saul McLeod, 'Pavlov's Dogs', Simply Psychology, (last updated 2018), https://www.simplypsychology.org/pavlov.html

18. Arnold Bennett. How To Live On Twenty-Four Hours A Day. (Page 37)

19. Peter Moseley, 'Talking to ourselves: the science of the little voice in your head', The Guardian, (last updated 21st August 2014), https://www.theguardian.com/science/blog/2014/aug/21/science-little-voice-head-hearing-voices-inner-speech

20. PsychAlive, 'The Importance of Self-Worth', https://www.psychalive.org/self-worth/

21. Blair Decembrele, 'Encountering a Quarter-life Crisis? You're Not Alone...', LinkedIn, (last updated 15th November 2017), https://blog.linkedin.com/2017/november/15/encountering-a-quarter-life-crisis-you-are-not-alone

22. Shana Lebowitz, 'From the projects to a $2.3 billion fortune – the inspiring rags-to-riches story of Starbucks CEO Howard Schultz', Business Insider UK, (last updated 30th May 2015), http://uk.businessinsider.com/rags-to-riches-story-of-howard-schultz-2015-5

23. David Sturt and Todd Nordstrom, '10 Shocking Workplace Stats You Need To Know', Forbes, (last updated March 8th 2018), https://www.forbes.com/sites/davidsturt/2018/03/08/10-shocking-workplace-stats-you-need-to-know/#7f3de57ff3af

24. Susan Greenfield. You & Me: The Neuroscience of Identity. (Page 15) & https://www.sparknotes.com/drama/bacchae/summary/

25. Shlomo Breznitz. Maximum Brainpower: Challenging the Brain for Health and Wisdom. (Pages 78-79)

26. Arnold Bennett. How To Live On Twenty-Four Hours A Day. (Page 41)

27. Canyon Ranch, 'How Your Brain Changes with Age', https://www.canyonranch.com/blog/health/how-your-brain-changes-with-age/

28. Sharon Begley, 'The Brain: How The Brain Rewires Itself', Time, (last updated January 19th 2007), http://content.time.com/time/magazine/article/0,9171,1580438,00.html

29. https://en.wikipedia.org/wiki/Warm-glow_giving

30. APA, 'In Rich and Poor Nations, Giving Makes People Feel Better Than Getting, Research Finds', https://www.apa.org/news/press/releases/2013/02/people-giving.aspx

CHAPTER FOUR

31. https://x.company & https://www.lifewire.com/google-x-secret-lab-1616267

32. https://en.wikipedia.org/wiki/Flickr & https://en.wikipedia.org/wiki/History_of_Facebook

33. Peter Fisk, Moonshot thinking, https://www.thegeniusworks.com/wp-content/uploads/2017/04/Moonshot-Thinking-by-Peter-Fisk-.pdf

34. Susan Greenfield. You & Me: The Neuroscience of Identity. (Page 100)

35. https://www.ted.com/talks/viktor_frankl_youth_in_search_of_meaning/discussion

36. Héctor Garcia and Francesc Miralles. Ikigai: The Japanese Secret to a Long and Happy Life. Hutchinson 2017. (Page 31)

About The Author

Jodanna Bird is a 28-year old British writer on a personal mission to make this crazy world a little easier to navigate. Aside from a colourful career in advertising and a degree in photography, Jodanna's next greatest achievement is studying to complete her unofficially recognised but very immersive qualification in 'Millennial Anguish' - her MA.

Using a mixture of first-hand experience, months of research and some wisdom from her Grandma, Jodanna is in the process of creating an entire collection of *"How to Survive"* books. She mixes psychological explanations with a smidge of humour to directly address life's puzzles and problems. And if that's not enough, she invites her readers to reach out and share their own mishaps and successes too.

A Gift To You

As a HUGE thank you for joining me on this survival journey, I want to offer you a special gift.

I have already started to write my next book, and now that we're friends, I would really love to get you involved.

How to Survive Being Single is an incredibly personable, humorous and REAL guide for anyone living life in the single lane. I am pulling together some insightful research to help us get to the nitty-gritty of singledom, as well as sharing stories of my own wins and woes for your personal entertainment. I am really excited about this one.

Visit **www.jodannabird.com** and enter your e-mail address to receive a snippet of Chapter One. If you enjoy the preview, send me your feedback, stories, insights and input on any of the channels below.

Together, I think we can make the next *How to Survive* book truly great!

STAY IN TOUCH:

Instagram @jodannabird
Facebook /jodannabird
E-mail hello@jodannabird.com

.

Made in the USA
Monee, IL
22 June 2020

34382933R00079